Tim Peeler is the Hunter S. Thompson of Southern poetry.

—Ron Rash, author of *Serena*

Some books don't fit into categories. And some poets don't. For a number of years now, Tim Peeler has been creating unique, character driven poetry sequences about folks who are neither proud nor ashamed of their poverty.

—Mike James, author of *Back Alley Saints at the Tiki Bar*

TRAP GAME

A Trilogy of Prose Poems

Tim Peeler

REDHAWK
PUBLICATIONS

Trap Game

Copyright © 2024 Tim Peeler

ISBN: 978-1-959346-65-4 (Paperback)

Library of Congress Control Number: 2024000000

Any references to historical events, real people, or real places are used fictitiously. Names, characters, and places are products of the author's imagination.

Cover: Tim Peeler, Robert T Canipe
Cover Photo; Jack Wells Dickson
Book design: Robert T Canipe

Printed in the United States of America.

First printing edition: 2024.

Redhawk Publications
The Catawba Valley Community College Press
2550 Hwy 70 SE
Hickory NC 28602
https://redhawkpublications.com

For Donald James Mackey

And Michael David Sparks

"Some people admire the work of a Fool,

For it's sure to keep your judgement cool;

It does not reproach you with want of wit;

It is not like a lawyer serving a writ."

—William Blake

"Who cares what games we choose,

Little to win and nothin' to lose."

—John S. Carter

Any resemblance to real people and incidents herein is the result of lunar gravity.

Contents

Every day it's a trap game

Vines waiting in crabgrass

The honest horror

Of seeing yourself

In the bathroom mirror

Something grabs your ankle

As you shuck your bones

From house to car

And then the road rises up

In an other than Irish way

Past hay fields of death

Your breath your breath

And your knowledge

The years you went to college

Then you cross a bridge

Of lockjaw fear

Without thinking or steering

The ghosts go with you

As you rage like Lear.

Frank Bidart once commented in an interview that an emphasis on voice isn't fashionable in contemporary poetry. That idea might go a long way towards explaining the lack of appreciation for Tim Peeler's work since Peeler's poetry is emphatically about southern voices and southern characters. Peeler is more original than fashionable. He is of the DIY, autodidact, mountain bred, and baseball referencing, fried bologna school of American poetry. He is also the only member.

Some books don't fit into categories. And some poets don't. For a number of years now, Tim Peeler has been creating unique, character driven poetry sequences about folks who are neither proud nor ashamed of their poverty. Peeler doesn't make a fetish of the blue collar. Poverty and wealth are just reference points. Economics is part of what defines his characters, but it is not the whole definition.

The emphasis on character is why Peeler is so hard to categorize. Though he is as southern as moonshine, pine trees, and molasses, his character-driven writing is closer to Chekhov than Dickey. He begins and ends with a person in a specific situation. There may not be a problem to solve, but there is definitely an incident to examine.

There is a texture to Peeler's poetry which comes from his deep knowledge and appreciation of vernacular. He can use words like "whatnot" and "fixin" and make them an integral part of the poem without drawing attention. He is not a flashy poet, but a subtle one. He draws the reader in and pulls rabbits out of every hat he comes across. He does this while making the reader care for characters who are often either left out of poetry or reduced to stereotypes. There are no "types" in Peeler's poetry. There are only people.

Many poets are addicted to the idea of the blazing line. They are in love with anthology pieces. Tim Peeler is not that type of poet. In his work, poetry happens as part of the everyday. It seems to be dictated from characters at a diner, rather than created by a solitary individual. This is not to say that the accessibility of Peeler's sleight-of-hand poetics is easy. He simply makes it look that way. His poems are as clear as mountain air and just as easy to take in.

—Mike James

RATH

He'd prop one boat foot

Against the brick porch wall

Lean back on his end of the bus seat

And say beauty is truth, truth beauty.

Punctuating the statement

With blue smoke blown

Out his nostrils like a horse

In the winter barn.

He had played for a team

Called the Celtics they said.

Almost seven feet tall.

He had to special order

His overalls they said.

Trap Game

I had played as well

Half his size

Though more like

A cur dog thrown

In the pit for sport

I was happy if

My head knocked

Into somebody's

Diving for a free ball

Elbowing the gut

Of a shooter

Driving a breakaway

Into the block wall

Of every old gym.

No beauty,

Only truth.

He come over

To help us shell peas

We listened to NASCAR

On the radio

Watched the traffic pass

He said:

There's a difference

Between knowing

And believing

I said you mean like

When we come up

Across the hayfield

And I'm lying top

On my backside

To poke the electric wire

With a pine stick

So we get under,

Knowing I might

Get killed believing

That I won't.

Yeah, he spit

And hit

The butcher bucket,

Stained red

With rabbit blood.

Trap Game

We'd gone to Traphill
To climb on the rock.
Stopped the gravel road
To snap Rath's picture
Front of a corn field
Tallest corn
We'd ever seen
Rath helt his hand up
Like a preacher blessing
A circle of crows.

Famous people

Posing together

In the breeze

Outside the stadium.

Goddamn those assholes.

Trap Game

Rath hired me on his landscape crew

When I was seventeen.

I was charged with the two-gallon

Glass jug of nasty yellow jelly

I'd mix in the backpack canister

I carried most days spraying

Whatever he instructed me to kill.

Rath give me a pair of White Mules,

Some amber colored safety glasses,

And the keys to an old state dump truck

That he called Maybellene.

I loved killing stuff

And driving that truck.

Rath was my uncle

Though my daddy,

A runt like me

Was not really his brother.

Momma said

It was complicated,

Something she liked to say

About a lot of things.

Trap Game

For a while Uncle Rath dated

A Hollywood actress they call Rose.

She was famous for a movie

Called Sex Lives and Videos.

Momma would not let me watch it

But Uncle did and it wasn't much,

But I saw why he was taken with her

Even if he was too old for her.

She was from that place down yonder

Where they have a water tower

That looks like a peach.

I'd kill every goddamn weed

In Cleveland County

If I could go out with something

That looked like Rose.

A couple days a week

I'd drive Maybellene

Over to this trailer park

At Conover and pick up

The Mexican lawn crew.

Four of them

Rode on the back

Smoking rolled up cigarettes

And hollering Hey Mommy

At any good looking girl

We might happen upon.

They wore red head rags

And so did I,

And sometimes at a job

The client would think

That I was one of them

And try out

Their high school Spanish.

I'd just nod

And go back to

Getting the mowers

And the weeders

Off the trailer.

Trap Game

The dumbass Hereford bull
That stepped on my foot
Looked out the feedlot gate
Every time a horseshoe
landed against the stake.
The pit beside the barn
Worn flat from our steps
Between the iron stobs.
When Rath thew, the shoe
Fell from the sky,
An act of God I swear.
Above us, the sun
Passed on its slow swim,
And Rath's afternoon shadow
Towered more than him.

I played the second half of a game

With my chin busted open.

The coach mashed a towel

Against it, then a piece

Of white medical tape

The blood oozed through.

I looked up in the stands

And saw Rath, stern-faced

As an Indian or a mortician.

After the game

He drove me to a friend's place,

A doctor Billy Jack,

Dressed in a buckskin shirt

And cowboy boots,

Who poured me a shot

Then stitched my chin

From side to side.

Trap Game

Turn off a mountain highway

Onto a paved chuck of road

That winds upward,

Narrows as it climbs

Toward the sunrise,

Becomes gravel

Then packed dirt,

Leading to the

Mansion in the sky.

Unload and watch

The Mexicans charge

Through the mist

On Dewalt standers,

Carving the five-acre yard

While I poison

The perimeter.

A man with a gun

Watches us from a window.

I was sitting on the porch
Watching the traffic pass
And talking to Rath who sat
In the yard on his tractor
Looking like a big ole bear up there.

There ain't nothing
Ever gonna happen around here,
I said, kind of mournful.
Always something gonna happen,
Rath replied, and I saw

His eyebrows raise and drop
Like his whole face had moved.
I don't know what I want to do.
I said. He knew my poison days
Had a expiration date.

Trap Game

The Mexicans weren't from Mexico.

They came from Guatemala.

Shorty was a tall hawk-nosed guy

With his eyes nearly on the sides of his face.

He told me that when he walked across the border

They caught him and took him back.

A week later he crossed again

And caught a bus here where his brother lives.

They don't mess around at work.

A job is something to be done

As fast as possible

Even if it's something

You don't really know how to do

Like cutting up trees

With chainsaws.

Rath calls them

The flying chainsaw circus.

Hanging from one limb

While they cut another,

Sideways, nearly upside down.

Rath pays them three an hour

More than anybody else.

I play Rath one on one.

He is sixty-eight

And stationary as a tree.

I back off from him

To get my mid-range shot,

My only real shot.

He only moves a step.

His go-go-gadget arm

Looms up and out,

Swatting my shot.

He dribbles twice,

Turns at the foul line.

Then comes forward,

A one hand shot

Like on an old youtube vid.

The ball barely touches the net.

I dribble around him

Far to his left.

Keeping my body

Between him and the ball.

His arm snakes around me,

Slaps the ball away.

I retrieve it.

He does it again.

Trap Game

Afterwards, he tells me

About a guy named George Mica,

Like the shiny rock on the mountain,

Said people thought he was slow,

But he struck like a cobra.

You didn't even see it.

Till he was going the other way.

If he was better than you,

I'd liked to see it, I said.

There's no end to the better

That's out there, he said.

After the slaughter

Rath stood on the court

Looking at the goal

And something beyond it.

He reminded me

Of the Indian

In Cuckoo's Nest.

Juicy Fruit, I said,

Breaking his trance,

And for once,

He laughed.

Something happened.

The mountain town cops

Showed up at our worksite.

We'd been hired to clear

A prime two-acre piece of land

For a Florida writer's vacation mansion.

There were four of them,

Straight from the university's

Criminal justice program,

Crewcut white boys

Pumped full of steroids.

They arrested us quickly

And headed back to town

Without a word

Of what we'd done.

Later I found out

A coed had accused

Our crew of assaulting her.

Trap Game

Rath knew everyone of consequence

In that town and had us out

And back home by the end of the day.

I was so grimed and burnt at that point

That the cops thought I was a Mexican too.

I was okay because I knew it was bullshit,

But the crew was terror-struck.

Next day they were nowhere to be found.

Rath's full first name was Rathbone.

He told me nobody called him that

Except for his long-dead mother.

And his high school basketball coach.

He had played for an all-white mill hill

High school team just before Korea.

Rath was the tallest kid in school history

As well as conference history.

The guy who owned the Chevy dealership

Gave him a new car his senior year.

His coach was a baldheaded retired

Marine sergeant with dark black rings

Around his eyes and a nasty scar

On the left side of his face.

He blubbered incoherently

In the team huddle

And the local papers

Said he was a genius.

Rath said he was a pall bearer

At Coach's funeral and by then

He didn't weigh nothing.

Trap Game

Cordie lived in the village,
The prettiest girl at the high school
Whose team name, the Royals,
Was a bit of optimism,
If not unvarnished irony.
Rath won the battle for Cordie
Over the quarterback from
Their six-man football team.

Cordie was embarrassed
By the outhouses, the lack
Of running water or electricity
In the houses on the hill
Above the river, all the boys
In overalls, chickens and pigs
Running everywhere.

Rath liked the hill, liked the people,
Who packed the gym on Friday nights.
He was drawn to the drunks
And the poker games and
The tough guys who worked on cars.
Rath's daddy was a lawyer.
Cordie's daddy was a fixer.

Maybe we are all floating down a river

Imagining this life, drinking beer

From coolers tied to inner tubes.

Maybe the whole hot mess

Is an illusion: the good the bad,

Love and loss, war and poverty,

Just plot points in movies

That play across our brains.

Hard work and passion,

Families and friends,

The fucking Internet,

Brokenness and loneliness,

Especially loneliness,

Because how can we be lonely

If we are all floating together

Down this river?

Trap Game

Rath doesn't like to talk about Cordie.

The one that got away.

But there are lots of stories.

People like to talk about their heroes.

And Rath was a hero.

And Cordie was too

For every poor girl

With big dreams.

Rath always thought

She'd come back for him,

And he waited,

Making his own buzz

Along the way,

Building a kingdom

Fit for a queen.

And now

He was an old man.

Stay positive and be still inside,

Rath told me as he walked me

Into the mountain town police station.

I was required to stand in a lineup

While the victim decided

If one of us had assaulted her.

You know you didn't do anything.

Rath was dressed in his country lawyer suit.

Cowboy hat and all.

The Mexicans were long gone

Though they hadn't done nothing either.

I was as scared as I'd ever been.

It's like going to the foul line

At the end of a game.

Take yourself out of it.

They led me to a door.

Then I was through it.

Trap Game

There were five of us.

The room smelled like

A freshly oiled floor at first.

Then it smelled like sweat

And fear, the way I smelled

Waiting for a beating

From my tired daddy.

We stood there

Side eying each other.

Regular looking guys

In work shirts and jeans.

I tried to think of a prayer

But I didn't believe in God.

A doughnut king's new mansion
Stood at the top of the hill.
The mountain town where
Robert Redford and Michael
Both owned a house.

Rath had hired more Mexicans.
One of them, a short stocky guy
With arms like Popeye the Sailor
Claimed he'd pitched to MLB guys
In a game in Mexico City.

He liked to throw rocks
At the other workers
When they weren't looking.
About the third time he hit me
In the shoulder while I was weed eating,

I grabbed him by the collar
Of the sleeveless work shirt
He'd picked from a dumpster,
And said, Rath will have someone
To slit your throat tonight.

He backed the hell off,
Apologizing, apologizing
In his Guatemalan jabber,
Terivio, Terivio, you know
That we all love you.

Trap Game

Rath watched the crew
Hauling fifteen-foot trees
From one ten-foot terrace
To the next, lowering them
Into the huge holes they'd dug.

I stood beside him,
Always amazed by the mad pace
That the Mexicans kept.
Trees, trees, Rath said.
The most important thing

That you can do in life
Is to plant trees. I guess,
I replied. I mean it. Why
Do you think I have this business?
To plant trees, that's why.

I'm telling you, Terivio,
Even he'd taken to the name,
When you get to heaven,
There's only one question they'll ask:

Did you plant trees?

The Mexicans called me Terivio.

I asked what it meant.

They said Little Bull.

One day they said Bullshit.

Later I asked a woman I met

When we were mowing at Centro Latino,

And she said she never heard the word.

Then I started asking every bilingual I met.

No one was for sure what the name meant,

But I liked the sound of it better

Than the sound of my plain ole redneck name.

Terivio, I practiced it at the morning mirror.

Trap Game

The road ended in a sweeping
Uphill right turn.
Then the gravel drive
Up up up
Between grandfather oaks
Into the blue sky,
Finally outside the three car
Basement garage.

I stopped the dump there,
The lawnmower trailer shook
In the deep gravel.
We got our stuff off
And four hours later
We finished the craziest
Three-acre estate
In the whole Blue Ridge.

The Mexicans drank
Some yellow concoction
From reused water bottles.
While I checked for a cell signal
The old man I called Hemingway
Came out the back door
Bear swaggering toward me,
All gray beard and yellow teeth.

Don't want you boys turning
Round in my yard, he said.
I'm tired of paying good money
To have my place fucked up.
Just as quickly he stomped back
To his house where he slammed
The door, grumbling all the way about
Half breeds and retards.

The Mexicans had the equipment loaded
By the time I finished looking
At the hill where it disappeared below.
The three of them had heard the old fart;
Two were in the back of the truck and one
Riding shotgun. You got this shit, Terivio,
They said, as I cranked and looked back
Over my right shoulder.

The gravel crunched as we creeped backwards.
Right baby, right the two shouted
From the truck bed. You got this shit.
You got this shit. Beyond them, blue sky.
I prayed to my grandpa and grandma.
I prayed for God to send somebody
To come up this mountain
And kill that old man.

Trap Game

Cordie came to visit one summer.
She stayed with Rath and acted
Like nothing had ever happened.
Her granddaughter came with her
Blonde and perfect as granny
In those movies she made
Back in the 70s.

I sat with her and lied
About what I knew about horses,
About cities I'd traveled to;
I'd never been nowhere.
I lied about my knowledge
Of the existential nature
Of Pink Floyd's lyrics.

Sylvia acted like she was interested
And she kissed me
When everybody left the room.
She told me she thought
I might just be her soulmate
And I believed it when she said it,
Right up to the end of that long weekend

When she and Cordie were suddenly gone
Without so much as a good-bye.
 Mark my stone

Was one of Rath's
Favorite things to say.

Mark my stone
He told me at the end
Of that summer

It's time for you
To get back
Into the game.

I wasn't sure
That I knew
What he meant.

Mark my stone
He told the woman
In the registrar's office

At the mountain college.
This young man is right
For this place.

Trap Game

Rath drove the lawnmower truck that day,

Dropped me off at the college

To go get a schedule.

As I got out dressed in my work clothes,

I looked back at the Mexicans

In the back of the dump truck,

Peering anxiously over the side at me.

You got this shit, Terivio, one of them said.

Hey mommy. Hey mommy another yelled

At a passing coed. I wanted to go with them.

To watch them do whatever crazy shit they would do.

To load my tank with poison and kill weeds like the devil while I watched.

I waited an hour in a line,

Talked to a woman at a computer

About classes and whatnot.

I waited an hour in another line

To give them Rath's fancy check.

I waited a hungry hour

To get my picture made.

Not one for lines,

I nearly left a couple times.

Hell I was twenty-four,

And all around me were kids

Carrying Daddy's credit cards.

Trap Game

Rath had said
We'll meet you back here at three.
Walk around, talk to folks.
Go see where your classes are.
By one o'clock I was whipped.
I strolled out the last building,
Wandered across a grassy field
Between rows of other buildings,
Found a sunny spot on a hill
And laid down.

I fell asleep and dreamed
That I was poisoning
All the grass on the campus.
I was told I would be awarded
A degree when it all died.

Around two I startled awake
Wondering where the hell I was at.
There was a young woman
To my left, sitting against a backpack
And reading a paperback.
She wore little round sunglasses
And her braided brown hair
Was pulled to either side.
She looked incredibly comfortable
But her brow furrowed as she read.

When she realized I was looking at her,

She smiled and said,

I saw you earlier.

You look like you might need some help.

That is probably true, I said,

Wincing at the sunlight

Streaming across her.

Maybe I'm still dreaming, I thought.

She was still smiling.

What's your name? she asked.

I looked around

To make real sure she

Was talking to me,

Cleared my throat,

Squared my shoulders,

And said, Terivio.

WHERE LIONS PROWL

He couldn't write unless he was hungry,

I couldn't write unless I was full,

And there we were sitting beside each other

At the coffee shop open mic,

Waiting to see who would win

The open mic lottery and

Get to read a bunch of poems

Instead of just one.

The tension was incredible.

You could feel the air vibrate in the waiting.

I had grabbed a stack of EntertainmentActives

With my baseball poems

Each week on page three,

Me being a real writer and all.

He had a spiral notebook filled

With his chicken scratch

And his little primitive pictures.

He claimed to be the southern Bukowski,

Had the drunk every night part down,

Was working on the rest.

So there we were beside each other

At the same coffee shop table

Pretending to be friends,

Waiting and hating each other

As the moderator

Who was a well-known designer

Of relatively insignificant designs,

Or so we thought,

Held our collective breath

In his hesitation—

Trap Game

We were both so certain

It would be us—

I was so full

And he was so hungry,

But then it was the goddamn Irish man

Who'd already drank five pints

Before he arrived,

And we knew he'd read

From here to County Clare,

So we got up and left

Transporting our art to the other coffee house

The one owned by wiccans

Where I would be his rodeo clown

And he would be my picador

In our movable feast.

2

Baseball is a metaphor for life, I said,
And allowed it a minute to sink in.
The audience clicked their fingers and hissed.
Okay, so they're getting it, I thought.
Among the crowd was a gorgeous redhead.
She wasn't smiling at me,
But it seemed like she might.
I began reading a poem about Phil Niekro.
I said he threw butterflies
Which I thought monumentally clever.
Three guys in the back clicked their fingers again.
But I doubt a soul in the room
Knew what a knuckle ball was
Or how it weaves and drops
On its spinless flight toward home plate.
The redhead looked down at her feet.
I grabbed another EA
And flipped to page three.
Y'all don't know who I am, I said.
They clicked their fingers again.
I read my version of Casey at the Bat
In which Casey does not strike out.
The wiccan who ran the show
Said sorry but your time is up.
I continued to read another,
A timeless, passive-aggressive open mic move.
I glanced over at my picador.
He was hunched over,
Biting his fingernails,
Waiting for his turn to read.

Trap Game

3

It was my picador's turn.
I poked him in the ribs
As he seemed comatose
And the audience of hipsters,
Goths, wiccans, and punks
Was hanging fire.
He struggled to his feet,
Muttered something
About the lost children
Of this good night
And began flipping pages
In his spiral notebook.
A minute or two crept by.
The three miscreants in the back
Began snapping their fingers.
I swear they had seen a Dobie Gillis
Episode on Hulu.
Pic mumbled again
Like he'd been drinking
Three or four days
And began his poem.
I'd gone to Hickory Speedway
With a crazy bitch I'd met
In the Wal-Mart parking lot.
We were drinking Orange Driver
And snorting some brownish-white powder.
Right there in the grandstand.
I had discovered that it was a car race,
Not a horse race.
The finger clicking commenced in earnest.
I threw up not once, but twice

On the people sitting in front of us,
And they called security on us,
But we were too smart for that shit
And hightailed it to the parking lot
Where we failed to locate my truck
Among the rows and rows and rows
Of trucks—I passed out, then woke up.
She'd left me with two guys
Who knew where their truck was.
And I crawled to the county cemetery
Across the creek from the race track
And stayed there for an entire week
Surviving by eating flowers off the graves.
Till I came here tonight.
Finger snapping filled the room.
Incense had been lit during the poem.
The audience beat their chests with their fists.

Trap Game

4

We sat through the horror

Of four or five more readers.

Critters of the dreariest sort.

I bought Pic a wiccan coffee

To keep him from nodding out.

When it was over

They announced their next month's events

And invited everyone to come back any time.

Afterward, my suspicions

About this crowd were confirmed.

Not a one approached me

To ask if I had a book for sale

So that I might explain that

I had one coming out soon.

In fact, many of them accosted Pic instead,

Begging him to tear a page out of his notebook

And sign it for them. One guy who had his hair

Arranged so that it looked like he had two horns

Gifted Pic five bucks. Another gave him a url

And told him there would be bitcoin waiting

For him there. Rubes, I thought,

A real writer here, right in their midst,

And they gravitate to the shyster.

5

But the night was hardly over.
I asked Pic if he wanted to walk
To the Irish pub and have a pint.
All right if she goes, he asked,
Nodding at the redhead
Who had attached herself to him
Shortly after the open mic.
We headed down the old
Main Street of the town
Crossing under and by
A flash of architectural wonder
Intermingled with modern ugliness.
Just before we reached the pub,
We were overtaken by a crew
Of goons stumbling up the sidewalk.
The first one held a huge bible,
And walked backwards reading from it.
He was closely followed by
A longhair in a robe
Who shouldered a heavy wooden cross.
Instead of a crown of thorns
He wore a Trump 2020 hat.
There were three or four others
Who scampered behind them
Like idiot cur dogs
Chasing a bit of action.
If you enter that bar,
The man carrying the bible
Shouted at us, you will burn in hell.
Burn in hell. Burn in hell.
The congregation chanted.

Trap Game

6

For a moment I was at a loss for words.

Then I looked at the Trump Jesus

And said, if I was ten years younger,

I'd beat you to death with that cross.

7

Once I had dismissed the Jesus hicks,
I could tell that the red head
Was looking at me differently.
We sat in one of those half shell
Wooden stalls in the underground pub.
From where I sat, I could see half of a TV
And hear all of the squalling
From the digital jukebox.
Pic was low key.
He sat quietly
Fingering his braided beard.
But halfway through the first pitcher
I could see his eyes change.
When he spoke, his voice deepened.
The red head looped her bare arm
Around him, but it was obvious that
Her coy smile was meant for me.
She asked us if we'd read Kerouac.
And of course she was shocked
To discover that his mother used
To babysit me when I was a kid
In Rocky Mount. You don't really
Have to make a move sometimes,
Just be connected.
At some point we decided to throw darts
And when we walked to the back area
Of the bar, she looked up at me
As if she was measuring me
For something later.

Trap Game

8

Pic was about to
Throw a dart
When suddenly
Mesmerized by
the string of green
Leprechaun lights
Along the ceiling,
He said
Pontotoc, Mississippi,
Is the most poetic
Southern name—
The natives knew how to
Cut some words.
The red head slipped her hand
In his back pants pocket
And said, Oh honey.
He had some kind
Of charming ignorant gravity—
That was for sure.
But he couldn't throw darts,
And I cleaned him up fast.
On the way back to our table,
I noticed a famous retired
Race car driver
Sitting with his wife and grown son.
I stopped long enough
To let them know
I was a published writer.
They attempted to ignore me

Till the red head grabbed
Me by the arm and pulled
Me along—never liked
Those NASCAR guys anyway—
No real athletes in that sport.

Trap Game

9
We'd been back at our table a while
When one of my students stopped by
Supposedly to chat—he was the son
Of the CEO at the largest case goods
Manufacturer in the area,
A tall goofy smart kid with serious problems.
Mind if I use your ashtray he asked,
And stood there, glassy-eyed,
Stubbing his cigarette,
Stone-still as a statue.
Are you okay, I asked.
He failed to answer.
Pic measured the room
With his raised monkey arms
And growled, these are my people.
I spotted another youngin
From the school and asked
Are you with him?
He came over and asked
What the hell is he doing?
Using our ash tray, I think.
Ambien, the other one said.
He passed out at a stoplight
Last night, but the cops
Took him home when
They saw who it was.
Get him away, I said.
And he did.

10

The red head, whose name

Turned out to be Kayren

Was suddenly screaming

At me to do something.

I think I had experienced

One of those brief brown out moments

Where I had travelled to another place.

In the meantime,

Pic had grabbed one of the patrons

By the collar, a gray bearded old guy

Who I recognized as the

Retired community theater director.

Give me my poems back

He hollered over and over.

There was a Lynyrd Skynyrd song

Blaring from the jukebox

And Pic was somehow

Keeping time with it

In his bellowing.

I have to admit:

He is not without talent.

In a few lunatic minutes

Myself and two other patrons

Wrassled Pic into submission.

Trap Game

11

It seems my fellow poet

Thought his notebook of poems

Had been snatched

While we were throwing darts,

But then in a quieter moment,

When he and Ronnie Van Zant

Had finished their spirited conjunction,

He realized he had left it,

Not on the table

But in the coffee shop.

Oh my goddamn, he said.

We got to go over there now.

They're closed, I said.

Don't matter, he replied.

Those aren't just poems;

They're also spells he continued.

Somebody else get a hold of them words,

We could all be in big trouble, he added.

This was obviously headed

Toward something bad,

And Kayren took this as a sign

That she had to get up early tomorrow.

Every midnight drunk in the place

Watched her ascend the wrought iron

Spiral stairs that led above to the street.

12

I may have suffered another one of those brown outs.

I recall telling Pic that Satchel Paige threw a pitch

Called the Pea Ball that actually got smaller

As it approached the plate.

That is magic, I told him, getting into somebody's head,

But I don't believe he followed my thinking.

Next thing I knew

We were standing in front of the coffee shop.

At the other end of the block.

We faced a dark wall of glass

With moons and flying saucers on it

As well as whatever their witchy name was--

I can never remember.

You could see our reflections

And the street behind us.

We looked bad—like the first page

Of a Faulkner novel.

Pic wanted to extract

One of the patio tables

From the sidewalk

And fling it through the window.

Trap Game

13

He tested each of them

Till he found one, a bit wobbly

And began shaking it back and forth.

I looked up and noticed

The full moon for the first time--

Should have known.

My days in the motel business

Taught me this lesson a long time ago.

A lesson I never learned.

I looked back

When I heard a crash.

The poet had somehow done it.

He'd shaken a table loose

And tossed it through the window.

Pic, you goddamn fool, I shouted.

Luckily, no alarm sounded.

Pic was examining the hole he'd made,

Trying to figure out

How to shimmy through it

With the least number of lacerations.

14

I believe that Pic had drugged me

Because the next thing I knew

I was inside the shop

Looking back out

Through the hole at him.

What I could see of his face

Was grotesque, crazed,

The Billy Goat Gruff

From the tale

My mother used to tell me

When she was giving me

My Saturday morning crewcut.

I spelled you in there, he said.

Now get my notebook

Over yonder where we sat.

Hurry, before the cops get here,

Throw it out to me.

Trap Game

15

It was dark in there--
A single night light burned
Behind the coffee bar.
I looked around some,
Found the table,
Nothing there.
I don't see it, I hollered at him.
On the floor
Under the table, he exclaimed
As if he'd already seen it there.
I got it, I said,
Scooping it up.
It felt fragile
Like a hundred-year-old book.
A couple papers fell out.
I grabbed them too,
Ran toward the window
And chunked them out.
I didn't hear a thanks.
I didn't hear anything,
Except a far-off siren,
Which I assumed
Was heading this way.
I slipped out the door,
Pushing it back shut, locked.
No apparent alarm, thank God.

16

I trotted down the sidewalk

To the corner of Main Street,

Turned left.

Another fifty yards

And I was in my truck,

Cranked and headed west

Through town quick as I could.

I'll not be doing this stupid shit anymore

Once my book comes out

I told myself.

I imagined the endless attention it would bring,

How I'd be able to quit my thankless job,

Get caught up on alimony.

I saw myself, fielding calls from an agent,

Making ridiculous demands

For my book tour stops--

No brown M & Ms.

Trap Game

17

There was one more stoplight in town

Before I crossed over the interstate

And headed to the mountain shack.

I could see it a long way off.

Red, of course.

A vehicle sat waiting there,

A BMW sports car.

I pulled up close.

I was ready to get gone.

The light changed to green.

The BMW sat there.

I blasted the horn.

It still failed to move.

I could hear sirens coming

From two different directions.

I backed up,

Pulled around beside the car,

Whipping my truck left,

Crossing the interstate

On the sweet country road

That would lead me away

Into the night.

I only got a glance

As I passed,

But sure enough,

It was my student,

His head slumped

Against the steering wheel,

As the light went red

To green to red again,

And the full moon

Flooded the dirty street

With all its crazy love.

WHEN SPARKY CAME BACK

1

It wasn't like I wasn't expecting it.

Just never thought it'd take 39 years.

He must have been really dead.

He looked like the last time I saw him.

Forty July 4ths ago.

He and One-Armed Ed

Running wild all night in Greenville.

He had a job then at the med school.

He had cut his long frizzy hair,

But he still wore the flannel shirt

Over the black one-pocket t.

Official uniform of the 70s hippie freak.

Trap Game

2

Sparky and Ed would sit there
In his apartment, somewhere
In the utter sprawl of adult
Student housing, and carefully
Draw lines of coke on a mirror
That had been made to
Look like a Ouija board.
After they snorted
They'd fast talk about
All the times they'd had
Back home at the biker bars
Along the NC-SC state line.
Ed drove one of those cars
That looked like a tennis shoe
With the great big windshield.
Sparky said it made him
Feel like he was in a fishbowl.

3

I was outside when I noticed him
Sitting shotgun in my old truck.
About to haul a second load
Of briars and walnut sprouts
Hacked from a scuppernong vine
To the scrub woods next to the field.
I'd left the radio on the NPR station.
An 80s John Cougar song rattled
Through the 27-year-old speakers.
Later I thought Cougar might have
Summoned Sparky; that was the last
Music he recommended back in 82.
He prided himself on musical
Insider information; after all a
Violinist and trumpeter good enough
To be in a symphony orchestra
And in the university marching band.
I recalled the trumpet his mom
Had inscribed on the foot stone
We found at the lonely corner
Of a vast Gaston County cemetery
On a summer day as hot as this one.

He looked at me out the Ford's open window
And asked, How you doin' mother fucker?

Trap Game

4

It didn't hit me then,
The fact that I was 65,
Retired now a year and a half,
And he was just a kid.
It didn't hit me
Because inside
I was still a kid—
What did hit me
With that one line
Dripping in sarcasm,
Delivered in his
Impossible sidekick
Southern drawl,
I heard myself
Talking in the classroom,
At literary readings,
To my wife,
To my children,
To my dogs.
I had copied him
Out of laziness
Or possibly
To keep alive
My closest
College friend.
Okay, I said.
How you been?
I asked the dead man.

5

The light glinted off his glasses lenses,

Luminous, suns; his eyes,

Deep space planets behind them.

Same old shit, man.

Getting fucked over every day.

You missed everything, I said.

And nothing, he replied.

Bear with me, I said,

As I climbed into the cab.

The door moaning shut.

Thorns had stabbed through my gloves

And I had wiped blood in my moustache.

Trap Game

6

Are those blackberries, he asked,

Pointing at the briar patch

Between the edge of the field

And the beginning of the forest.

Haven't had those since

Daddy moved to his drug house

On the South Fork of the Catawba.

In the movies, the dead don't eat,

I commented from behind the truck bed,

Which I was about to empty

Onto the brush pile.

This one does, Sparky answered,

Reaching for a couple big fat berries.

The berries made his lips look bruised.

7

What happened to you, I asked
When we were back in the truck.
I talked to the guy at Papa Katz,
And I talked to your mother, too.
But I never got the story straight.

I slipped upon the floor and hit my head.
That's what all the angels said.
And he looked at me like he did
That one time I stole the beer he'd hid
In the very very back of the frig.

Trap Game

8

That last time I saw you
July 4th 82 I knew
You were not long for this,
But didn't want to say it.
Didn't want to fuck up the buzz.

We were living in a rent house
Not much more than this one
I said, pulling the truck beside
Our guest house/craft house,
When I called Papa Katz.

I wanted to tell you
We were expecting our first,
Eager to hear you say way to go, fucker.
But the guy who answered said.
Sorry, Dude. He's dead.

9

We sat on the front porch
Watching the traffic fly by.
He pulled a cigarette from a red pack.
Lit it in one smooth motion.
Still smoking those cowboys, I see.

I took a sip of an energy drink
And sighed as the breeze
Swept across the plank floor.
One time I wrote a list
Of all the things you missed.

You've become a morose old man,
He said. He still had his peach fuzz moustache.
I had a wiry white one that bristled
Like the briars in the grape vines.
Have you got any Stroh's? he asked.

Trap Game

10

Nobody has Stroh's or paneled walls
Or phone booths or card catalogues
Or straight drive transmissions.
I've got a Corona.
You've got a what.

We were watching the neighbor
Across the street drag a hose
Around his house to wash his car.
Kept dragging it, pulling it harder
But it never would reach his soap bucket.

Damn if that fucker's not coked up,
Sparky said, laughing to himself.
Hell no it's not coke, I said, handing
Him the icy Corona bottle.
A ghost that killed himself

Drinking and smoking, still at it.
Don't that just beat it all.
You've got it all wrong, he said.
I've switched it up.
Now I'm smoking and drinking.

11

A group of cyclists pedaled by,
Two lines shoulder to shoulder,
Ugly-faced and bent to their work.
The neighbors' dogs bark-bounced
From one end of the trailer to the other.

Sparky took a long hit on his Winston,
Eased up so the smoke emerged
From his nostrils, and somehow from his ears.
It was the dogs that killed me, man.
That's what I'm here to tell you.

He looked at me as he always had,
A young man's face, an old man's eyes.
I thought you fell in the bathroom,
Smashed your head on the toilet.
That's what the scorecard says.

The dogs across the street had moved
Back to their sentry posts and I thought they were watching us.
They can't see me, Sparky said, but they know
That I'm here. He tapped the smoldering butt
In the ceramic ashtray my wife made for this table.

Trap Game

12

It was the dogs at the med school lab
On the days that they met their maker.
I could smell death in the air when I walked in,
And I was of course hung over unless
It was late in the month. Then I was broke.

The company that supplied the animals
Had debarked them, so the sounds that
Came from those tortured bastards
Was nothing like a dog was supposed to make.
I moved around the lab in slow motion.

Setting up the stations for the students,
Trying to avoid eye contact with the animals.
But it was like they say about a car wreck.
You can't look away, and I took their fright
With me everywhere I went even after I quit.

And the med students and the profs
Looked at me with the same disdain
They held for the animals so that I never
Had any doubt that they would just as soon
Strap my ass to a table and cut me open, too.

13

God damn the pusher man, I said.
A tractor with a stacked hay wagon creeped by
Followed by a school bus and several screechy-
Braked dual-wheeled pickup trucks.
When I quit, the world was on my ass.

My parents were livid.
How could you leave your dream job?
The one you were trained for.
Marie, remember her, wouldn't speak to me.
The guy that helped me get the job, the same.

In the meantime, I got another DUI.
Lost my license for life, judge declared.
Whatever happened to Marie? I asked.
Her name was really Debbie, but we all
Called her Marie because she was Marie Osmond's double.

I'll get around to that.

Trap Game

14

I got the job at Papa Katz,
Booking bands and bartending,
And that crowd, they accepted me.
The college kids, all younger than me now.
I was always a scrawny little redneck

From Gastown, never had the girls,
But every night at PK's, I took them back
In the office and laid the lines of coke out.
Then we made the beast right there
With the music blaring out in the bar.

All the noise covered up the sound of those dogs,
And I forgot their eyes,
Watching myself in streaked-up mirrors,
And I forgot Marie except the weekends
I went home to see her.

15

The owner let me drive his beat up truck,
And I'd leave Papa Katz at 2:30 small,
Hurtling through Pitt County darkness,
Hissing under street lights on 10th Street,
Arriving somehow at the house

On Cotanche that I shared with two coeds
I'd met during the summer.
PK paid me under the table,
The student loan sharks
Having lost track of old Sparky.

Darkness had fallen in the countryhood.
You could hear the tree frogs in the Mimosas
Where the barnyard met the field.
The ashtray was full and six Corona empties rowed
Beside Sparky's chair, just like old times.

Trap Game

16

I haven't told you about my girls.
I forget their names or rather
Their names didn't matter.
They had money and boyfriends
Back home that they forgot about, too.

I'd have one of them
Or both of them a couple times a week.
I listened to their shitty music
And watched soap operas with them
In the afternoons.

I couldn't hear the dogs anymore,
But I sensed that I was partaking
In the forbidden fruit, yet there was
Always another night and by the third beer
And the fourth line, it was Dear Mr. Fantasy.

I loved my girls in the nostalgic
Mercurial way that a coke fiend might.
As any romantic outlaw hiding in plain sight might.
I loved my girls. I loved my girls. I loved my girls,
But they were just using me.

17

Though I was mesmerized by his story,
I could not deny my old man exhaustion.
I carried my third energy drink with me
When I walked around the corner to piss.
You remember Toothpick Jones, Sparky hollered.

Yes, I answered as I zipped my jeans.
You're lying he said as I retook my seat.
I just made up that name. You lie too easy
He said. You might be lying about seeing me
Right now, he said, for all I know.

That's one reason I'm here, to tell you
To quit lying so much. It was lying that did me in.
I thought you said it was the dogs.
Dogs, lies, what's the difference
After thirty-nine years in the ground,

Riding the Earth as it turns like an eight ball
Rolling toward the corner pocket.
Now how's that for poetry. . .
I sighed and said I've gotta call it a night.
Wait, let me tell you about the last night, he said.

Trap Game

18

Sparky looked off into the distance
As if the story were coming on the train
We could hear across the river gorge.
It was dark as it is tonight,
And we'd closed the bar a little early,

Me and two moonlighting school teachers
Who waitressed and tended bar weekends.
A couple crazy bitches, married, but I'm not
Sure what kind of married, you know.
We were drunk and stoned and we'd done

Some lines in the office on the way out.
We had this game we played sometimes.
We'd take the golf clubs we kept for protection
And some pool table balls and play a round
On the Putt-Putt course next door to PK's.

I don't remember that much about it.
Except for beating the propeller
Off the windmill and one teacher woman
Pulling her pants down
To moon a passing driver.

19

It was February, freezing cold,
And we must not have lasted long.
Next thing I knew I was in the truck
Driving past the tennis courts and
Government housing on Hooker Road.

I don't know how I got to the house,
But I remember standing at the door,
Fumbling for the key, wavering drunk.
Then I got this idea, the way you do,
Wake one of the girls to get a little bit.

And BAM BAM BAM--I hit the door.
I waited a minute and hit it again.
Then I heard the lock click and the door opened.
The girl with the chunky ass was standing there
In an East Carolina football jersey.

Goddamnit Sparky, she muttered,
Turned and stumbled back to her room.
I heard her lock click behind her.
I was really fucked up.
The room was getting sideways.

99

20

I knew what I had to do.

I slumped back on the sofa,

Extracted the glass vial from my watch pocket

And laid out two enormous lines

On the glass topped coffee table.

I slurped them up professionally with a rolled up dollar bill,

Watched the pink explosions light the dim room

And felt the crescendo of pops in my aural passages.

Suddenly my bladder needed to release all that beer.

I stood and steadied myself with a hand on the table.

I felt the rush of heat from the oil furnace grate

As I crossed it pinball-ing through the hallway

Toward the unheated bathroom at the back

Of the house. When I opened the door,

The cold air rushed all over me.

I stumbled forward and fell.

Tim Peeler is a retired educator from Western North Carolina who has written twenty-two books of poetry, short stories, and regional history. He has twice been a finalist for the Casey Award for baseball book of the year, and five of his books are housed in library at the Baseball Hall of Fame in Cooperstown, NY. Most recently he has collaborated with the Appalachian photographer Clayton Young on books that combine verse narratives and rural images.

41960461R00062